to Mark
for your enjoyment
and benefit
John Y

It **Has** to be Better Than **THIS!**

Life Everlasting seen through the Eye of Faith

It **Has** to be Better Than **THIS!**

Life Everlasting seen through the Eye of Faith

Jay A. Young, Ph.D.

Allerton Press – Silver Spring, Maryland

Published by Allerton Press
12916 Allerton Lane
Silver Spring, Maryland 20904

Design and formatting: Thomas I. Kirkpatrick
Cover photography: Cecilia A. Kirkpatrick
Post-processing by Thomas I. Kirkpatrick
Artistic input and guidance from Antonia Young
Editorial Review: Rev. John L. Young, C.S.C., M.D.,
Steve Weber, Thomas Young

ISBN 978-1-105-54478-1

Preface

A long time ago Wisdom said[1]:

> From the greatness and beauty of created things their original author, by analogy, is seen.

Approximately 200 years later Paul said it this way[2]:

> In fact, whatever can be known about God is clear; he himself made it so. Since the creation of the world, invisible realities, God's eternal power and divinity, have become visible, recognized through the things he has made.

Our Creator is our lover. Lovers disclose themselves to their beloved. Whether or not we love him, he is continuously disclosing himself to us: in our sunsets, in our quiet moments, in the rainbow, in the wine we enjoy, in our neighbors, in his clouds, in the water we drink, in the image in the mirror, in our sorrows, in the seeds we plant, in our children, in the work we do, in a snowflake--this list has no end.

It is you and me; we are the reason it is not yet Better Than This. As the beloved it is our responsibility to show our lover that we love him.

In this book I have tried to look at a few of the details of our lover's disclosures and to suggest that through our love in return it will indeed become better than it is now.

Jay A. Young

Silver Spring, Maryland, USA

September 8, 2011

---

[1] Wisdom 13, 5

[2] Romans I, 19-20

Acknowledgments

I hope that all of the errors and just plain goofs that somehow appeared in earlier drafts have been corrected. For their helpful comments and corrections, but more particularly for their constructive suggestions, I wish to acknowledge the help of my sons and daughters, Rev. John L. Young, C.S.C., M.D., Commander Laurence M. Young, USN, Cecilia Kirkpatrick, M.S.P.H., Lucy Crouch, R.N., M.S.N. and Thomas Young, B.A. And also Thomas Kirkpatrick, B.S., Magen Broshi, Ph.D., Rev. Jonas D. Cristal, Rev. Msgr. Francis Kazista, M.A., Patrick McGovern, Ph.D., Victor Schneider, M.D., and Nancy Stein, R.N. For her editorial help and cogent suggestions I thank Lois Wilson, Ph.D. The influence of *Spe Salvi and Caritas in Veritate* is doubtless evident. Not least, but first of all, I appreciate the help, criticisms, and encouragement of my wife, Mary Ann, without whom this task could not have been accomplished.

All biblical translations are taken from the New American Bible, St. Joseph Edition, with the exception of the translation from Job on page 5, which is from the New Jerusalem Bible.

I am responsible for the errors and omissions that remain.

J. A. Y.

Foreword

The bible states that God created us in His image. What does this mean? How do we fit into His universe? Why are we here? Whether or not you consider yourself "religious" matters not. We have all pondered these questions.

Dr. Young wrote this book in an attempt to discuss answers with you, the reader. In it, he has brought to bear on this quest his lifetime of Christian faith, study of the Bible, and scientific knowledge. His intent: build a bridge of understanding and reconciliation between those for whom science is absolute truth and those for whom religion is absolute truth.

This is not an Agatha Christie mystery. Don't expect to finish reading this book on a flight from Dulles to SFO. You may find the author's words so full of insights and ideas that you will be saturated. You may feel the need to put the book down from time to time to give your mind a chance to ponder and process what you have read.

Dr. Young was an acclaimed lecturer and writer, whose clear and often witty mode of expression fully engaged the imaginations and minds of his audiences. He used his teaching gifts in the classroom, on television, and even in the courtroom, where juries have been known to applaud after his expert testimony made complex scientific matters understandable to them so they could render an informed verdict. So fear not. Forge ahead. Reap the rewards of this remarkable testament.

Thomas I. Kirkpatrick

Half Moon Bay, CA

Introduction

God has a big problem. For several centuries now God has been trying to tell us who He really is, that He does indeed love us, and why He allows terrible things to happen. The problem is that if He told us plainly, the information would be so astounding, so terrifying, so wonderful, that knowing what we would then know, the experience would destroy us. And that, we can all agree, would not be a good idea.

So what does God do instead? He does tell us but He speaks indirectly. In chapter **13**, verses 1, 4 and 5, the Book of Wisdom recommends that we examine the grandeur and beauty of our surroundings, contemplating in their features the hand of our Creator.

We have been slow in responding. What does He ask us to do?

Listen to the stars.
Savor the taste of a mango.

Listen to a beautiful sunset.

Hear the song of a bird.

Love those who are not very lovable (and everybody else too).

Attend to the silence of solitude.

Realize the melody of a storm.

I hope this small book will help us listen, and savor.

And also hear, attend, and realize.

But especially— help us all, everyone, to love

Contents

Our rainbow, arcs of red, orange, yellow, green, blue, indigo, and violet, is generated by our sun in combination with droplets of water in the air. Our sun is a star; other stars have rainbows too. In their rainbows our loving creator has disclosed a portion of the magnificence of his creation.

Water is a compound composed of two elements, hydrogen and oxygen. It is a unique compound in that all other binary (two-element) compounds of hydrogen are gases whereas under ordinary conditions water can exist as a gas, a liquid, and a solid. Scripture states (Proverbs 8: 29 and Job 38: 8-11) that water is somehow restricted. This chapter examines that restriction emphasizing that the result, water tends to be a liquid instead of a gas or solid, demonstrates God's love for us.

Why are old wineskins likely to rupture if they are used for the storage and/or transport of new wine? This is the only example of a "Do not do this." in Scripture that is not accompanied with the reason why the action is not recommended. With a brief meditation on this otherwise not very interesting topic.

On the satisfaction that results from learning and applying newly learned information, especially information related to our Creator's relationships with his creation–including us, his much-loved human beings.

Joseph's coat of many colors presaged Christ's white garment of his transfiguration. The difference between the two garments resides in the definition of the word, "white." Both garments were colored, Joseph's in ordinary colors, Christ's in transcendent, infinite, colors.

How can you tell whether an event is a miracle or not? What is a miracle anyway? Those priests of Baal certainly had no doubts when Elijah called upon the one God to burn the thoroughly water-soaked offering on the twelve-stone altar he built for the occasion. But what about miracles today? Does God still perform miracles?

Without words living beings, animals, plants, even stars, by their nature communicate with other plants, animals and stars.

We too are included, lovers do not need words to communicate. Our Creator is our lover, we two can communicate without words.

On the creation of the universe, what was created and how we, each one of us specifically, came to be resurrected stars. And if indeed while we live on this earth, we are stars that have been resurrected, then consider what it will be like when we are resurrected in our life to come.

While he was in his mother's womb, John the Baptist jumped for joy. We are in the womb of our present life awaiting our birth into eternity. Perhaps if we knew the reason why John jumped joyfully before he was born, we too here and now would also jump for joy.

We are not lost in an uncaring universe with no recourse against an unknowable fate. Quite the opposite: We have an all-powerful, all-loving Creator, who patiently waits for us to learn to love him in return.

A few explanatory notes addressed to the more scientifically/ mathematically sophisticated readers concerning a few statements in the text involving the physics of light and the exposition of very large numbers.

Beyond the Rainbow

I propose reality as the basis of hope. We live our lives encased in an evanescent reality, a reality destined to become unreal, to vanish. Because hope finds its basis in reality, it is necessary to recognize that beyond the reality in which we presently have our being there is an eternal reality, a reality that is even now so real that it generates reason for hope. Even now, things are a lot better than we ever thought they could be.

And they're going to get better yet!

The task is in the understanding. If we can understand our present reality differently, it is already better than we think it is. In the pages to follow, I propose to describe a few examples.

According to the story that one way or another almost everyone has heard, Noah was pretty old when it all happened. There was a big rain storm, bigger and more awesome than it ought to have been, and a lot of people drowned. Noah however, warned by God beforehand, had built an ark within which according to the story he hospitably cared for his family and for male and female pairs from all of the then existing non-human creatures that lived on the surface of the earth.

Then, after the storm there was a rainbow and we are told in the story that the rainbow was the sign of a promise, a promise made by God himself, that there would never ever be another big rainstorm like that one. Although the story is otherwise silent about promises, the rainbow was more full of promise than the story-teller knew. Beyond that rainbow lies another story, the story of a further reality, the story of the whole magnificent universe.

Like this:

Currently there are more than one-hundred known elements. Twenty (or twenty-two, depending on the definition you might prefer) are non-metals; the rest are metals. Most of the elements occur naturally, a few are artificial. The natural elements comprise the matter of which the earth, the moon, the other planets, and the sun, are composed. The names of some of the elements are familiar, others not as familiar: copper, iron, gold, neon, magnesium, aluminum, oxygen, chlorine, sulfur, thallium, platinum, iridium, cesium, praseodymium, radium, ytterbium, osmium, tungsten, iodine, selenium, seborgium, einsteinium and all the rest. Some of the elements that are present at high concentrations in a star or in our sun are present at lower concentrations in some of the other stars. The composition of one star is not necessarily the same as the composition of another star.

We know the elements of which the earth is composed principally by chemical analysis. We know the elements of which the sun is composed from the colors of the rainbow.

To explain, in a fireworks display the red color you see is caused by the calcium present in the fireworks. If the fireworks contain barium, the color is green. Thallium or copper produce blue; sodium produces yellow[3]; iron produces sparkling white. It is neon inside glass tubing that causes the red in a neon sign. Look carefully and you will see that the red that is characteristic of neon is a different shade of red from the fireworks red that is characteristic of calcium. The blue flame characteristic of copper is a different shade of blue compared to that of thallium.

Each element produces a color[4] that is unique for that element. The colors of the rainbow come from the light of the sun, separated into its components (that is, refracted) by the water in the raindrops, forming a visible arc of red, orange, yellow, green, blue, indigo, and violet in the sky. In the total spectrum of the rainbow we can detect each of the different spectra[5] of each of the elements that compose the sun.

---

[3] When a pot boils over, the flames of a gas burner are colored yellow from the sodium in the salt that the cook added to the pot.

[4] Strictly, a set of colors, with one (usually only one) color predominant.

[5] To do this we use various scientific instruments similar to (but more refined than) the successive rows of circular grooves in a CD-ROM or DVD disk. The incident

Similarly, in the total spectrum of a star, we can by diffraction detect the spectra of the elements of which that star is composed. Like the sun, each star has a rainbow and the rainbow of a star reveals the reality of that star. The rainbow of a star tells us which of the elements are in that star.

However, compared to our sun, the spectra of the stars are slightly different. The elements composing a star yield a spectrum of colors for the elements in that star that are slightly more reddish than the spectrum of colors produced by the same elements in our sun. This shift of colors is called a "red shift." Some stars have a greater red shift than other stars; and some other stars, a lesser red shift. The red shift is caused by the movement of the stars away from us here on earth[6]. Some of the stars are moving away from us at great velocities—a large red shift; some not quite as fast—a lesser red shift. The farther a star is from us, the faster it is moving away from us. (It is as though our earth and sun and the other planets have really, really bad breath, or something.) Furthermore, each of the stars and galaxies are moving away from each other at great velocities. It is as though the universe can be compared to a big balloon, with a large number of inked dots (each representing a star or galaxy) on the surface of the balloon, and someone is inflating the balloon causing each inked dot to become farther and farther away from its neighbors as the inflation continues.

When next you see a rainbow, look beyond the rainbow. Look to the further reality, the reality of the universe, revealed by the rainbow. Look beyond the reality of the universe. Visualize the eternal reality.

Hope depends upon a reality.

That reality cannot be seen, cannot be touched, cannot be felt, can only be imagined.

---

light shining upon a disk is diffracted (not refracted, which is a similar process) by the succession of grooves into the colors of which the incident light is composed.

[6] The sounds we hear can exhibit a similar phenomenon. Imagine that you are standing at an intersection and a passing automobile sounds its horn as it approaches and continues to sound while it passes you. As the automobile approaches, the pitch of the sound of the horn that you hear rises and after it passes by, the pitch you hear decreases.

Analogously, the same applies to the reality that we do discern. That is, beyond the easy to discern reality of the rainbow lies the more difficultly discernible reality of the stars in the universe.

And beyond the reality of those stars is the reality of the universe.

And beyond that *is* the hoped-for, indiscernible, wonderful, eternal reality.

Through prayer we strengthen our hope for that ultimate reality. The reality that now can only be imagined.

The Polarity of Water

Consider the words in Proverbs 8: 29: I was with him "When he compassed the sea with its bounds and set a law to the waters..."

Similarly, but in more detail, in Job 38: 8-11 "Who pent up the sea behind closed doors when it leaped tumultuous from the womb, when I wrapped it in a robe of mist and made black clouds its swaddling bands; when I cut out the place I had decreed for it and imposed gates and a bolt? 'Come so far,' I said, 'and no farther; here your proud waves must break!' ".

Water is a liquid, a solid (ice), and a gas (water vapor) under ordinary conditions. It is a compound of hydrogen and oxygen. All the other chemically related compounds of hydrogen and other elements are gases. Under ordinary conditions the compound of hydrogen and nitrogen, ammonia[7], is a gas. The compound of hydrogen and carbon, methane, is a flammable, explosive gas under ordinary conditions. Similarly, the compound of hydrogen and sulfur, hydrogen sulfide, is a poisonous gas characterized by a "rotten egg" odor. The compounds of hydrogen with phosphorus, boron, silicon, fluorine, and chlorine, all five, and still others not mentioned here; all are gases under ordinary conditions. To get these other gases[8] to condense into a liquid requires temperatures below 32° F (0° C). And to get any of those liquids into the frozen, solid, state, they must be chilled even further.

Gaseous methane, for example, liquefies at –260° F (–162° C); liquid methane freezes at –299° F (–184°C).

---

[7] The familiar household cleaning liquid known as "Ammonia" is a solution. It is composed of the gas that is properly called ammonia by dissolving it in water, often with a little soap or detergent, and perhaps a bit of perfume added.

[8] Except hydrogen fluoride, which condenses into liquid at 68° F (20° C). Liquid hydrogen fluoride freezes at –116° F (–83° C).

Water is the only common substance that can exist under ordinary conditions in three forms: gas, liquid, and solid. Liquid water is familiar to everyone. Almost everyone is familiar with ice. Water vapor is invisible but in cold weather the water vapor in our exhaled breath is cooled and forms droplets of liquid water so we say that we "see our breath" as the droplets of mist in our now cooled, exhaled breath. Fog consists of innumerable tiny droplets of water that have formed from chilled water vapor near ground level. Clouds are the result when the same thing happens at higher elevations[9].

None of the other closely related compounds of hydrogen exist in three forms in the same way that water does. Why is water different?

There was more to the rainbow than that which we first observed. There is more to water as well.

"Aitch-two-oh", H_2O. Almost everyone knows the formula for water. Briefly put, a molecule of water is a combination of three atoms, two atoms of hydrogen and one atom of oxygen, symbolized by H_2 for the two atoms of hydrogen and you would think, O_1 for the one atom of oxygen. But to keep things as uncluttered as possible, it was agreed long ago that if only one atom was involved, the subscript, "1", would be omitted, so it is H_2O for a molecule of water.

Atoms are exceedingly small. Think of an atom as a sort of little ball. If you line up a bunch of hydrogen atoms, all in a line, to make a line of hydrogen atoms that is one inch long, that would take approximately 8.2×10^{10} hydrogen atoms[10]. Comparatively, oxygen atoms are about five times larger in diameter so for a line of oxygen atoms one inch long, approximately 1.6×10^9 atoms[11] are required.

Water molecules have a shape, like the letter "V," but spread out a little more so that the angle between the arms is approximately 105°. The oxygen atom is at the bottom of the "V" and the two hydrogen atoms are, one each, at the ends of the arms of the "V." Like this:

---

[9] A typical cumulous cloud contains several tons of water droplets.

[10] 82 billion hydrogen atoms

[11] 16 billion oxygen atoms

(a)   (b)

Figure 1. (a) A schematic representation of a molecule of water emphasizing the angular details among the atoms of the water molecule. (b) This schematic emphasizes the shape of a water molecule—a larger sphere with two embedded spherical "ears".

Now this is the important point: Each of the hydrogen atoms in the water molecule has a small positive electrical charge while the oxygen atom has a small negative electrical charge. *Positive and negative charges attract each other. Similar electrical charges, positive and positive, and negative and negative, repel each other.*

In liquid water the individual molecules of water attract each other. They cling together forming clusters of individual molecules, like this:

Figure 2. A typical cluster of water molecules in liquid water. The three short black lines represent the plus-minus attractive force between the hydrogen and oxygen atoms in the adjacent molecules.

In the clusters, oxygen atoms (with a negative charge) of an individual molecule are close to one of the hydrogen atoms (with a positive charge) of another molecule. The clusters are constantly moving about in liquid water, some clusters move at high speed, some very slowly, and some at intermediate velocities. They bump into each other. In an ordinary 6 or 8 ounce glass of water there are approximately 1.6×10^{23} clusters[12] colliding with each other more frequently each second than the total number of all people who have lived since the first human beings drew pictures on the walls of their caves.

In some of these collisions the colliding clusters are entirely broken up into individual molecules and in other collisions there is less damage with, say, two or three, or only one, molecule lost. In any event, the freed molecules will re-join their clusters, or form with other free molecules to make new clusters. Or, if a lone molecule happens to be directed upward and is near the surface and traveling at sufficient speed, it will escape from the liquid (it evaporates) and becomes a gas molecule; it becomes a molecule of water vapor.

Also, within a cluster the molecules are constantly moving about, like a wiggling snake. Occasionally two oxygen atoms on two different molecules in the same cluster happen to get near each other. In such an instance, because of minus-minus repelling, one of the two molecules involved is likely to be repelled out of the cluster. Sooner or later, that lone repelled molecule joins a cluster or instead evaporates from the liquid water.

The opposite, plus-plus repelling, occurs when two hydrogen atoms on two different molecules happen to get too close to each other in a cluster. And again, one of the two molecules involved could be repelled out of the cluster.

As we have seen, evaporation takes place at the surface. But boiling is different, it occurs within the bulk of the water usually near the bottom of the container of water—near the source of heat.

Water boils[13] at approximately 212° F, depending on the atmospheric pressure (for example, the elevation above or below sea level). Instead of single fast moving molecules near the surface, several millions (or

---

[12] 16 followed by 22 zeroes

[13] Strictly, pure water boils at 212° F . If the water contains any dissolved salt or sugar, for example, the boiling point at sea level, etc., is greater than 212° F. At elevations above sea level, on a mountain, for example, the boiling point of pure water is less than 212° F and the boiling point of water containing a dissolved substance is similarly altered.

more) molecules that happen to be near each other and happen to be moving fast in more or less the same direction form a bubble of steam within the liquid water. If it is large enough to be easily seen, a bubble of steam contains approximately 20,000,000,000,000,000,000 individual (not congregated) molecules of water[14]. In that bubble, the individual molecules would be moving about, hither and thither, bouncing against each other, at speeds from zero to up to several hundreds of miles an hour.

In both steam and liquid water the hydrogen atoms in the individual water molecules are vibrating away from and toward the oxygen atoms. It is a stretching and relaxing, repetitive movement, as though the hydrogen and oxygen atoms were attached to each other by springs that are continuously being alternately stretched and compressed. The higher the temperature, the more vigorous the action.

To summarize, this is liquid water: Individual molecules in the clusters of 3 to 5 (on average) molecules are continually leaving one cluster and joining another cluster. Meanwhile, the clusters themselves are moving about at lesser velocities (compared to the velocities of individual molecules in steam) bouncing against each other. These go off from those collisions in all directions, with the atoms in their individual molecules stretching and relaxing, generally mixing it up, we might say. They move more rapidly at higher temperatures and more slowly as the water cools, merely vibrating when the water freezes at 32° F.

Water freezes at 32° F and below this temperature the ramming into each other and the leaving of one cluster to join another, all this, stops. Only the spring-like stretching and relaxing movements continue, and even these at a slower frequency than it was in the liquid water.

Consider snowflakes; in a single snowflake there are approximately 1,000,000,000,000,000,000 molecules[15] each one stretching and relaxing in position like dancers in a choreographed exercise. Like this: imagine

---

[14] In order to understand the magnitude of the number, 20,000,000,000,000,000,000, (20 pentillion) of water molecules in a single small bubble of boiling water, we can consider the same number of bricks. That number of bricks would cover the entire surface, including the oceans, lakes, rivers and ponds (as though the bricks could float) of 1,000 planets the same size as the earth. See the appendix for the details of the calculation that proves this statement.

[15] 1 billion billion or 10^{18} molecules

hexagons, like floor tiles, arranged each next to the other to cover the floor. Imagine an oxygen atom at each corner of every hexagon, with two hydrogen atoms near each oxygen atom. Now on top of the tiled floor imagine another layer of hexagons with oxygens and hydrogens as in the first layer. And then another similar layer, and another layer, and another, and so on for more layers than we could count, and their hydrogen and oxygen atoms all dancing as choreographed. Only in the few layers near the surface are the molecules free to move about a bit and occasionally get bumped with sufficient force to leave.

The polarity of water is fundamental. Without it, the clusters could not exist and water would be a gas under ordinary conditions. The polarity reduces the volatility of the H_2O units (molecules), they become liquid water. And consequently life as we know it becomes possible.

That is the beginning of the story of water; the complete tale would more than fill a few books. The words in Proverbs and in Job suggest that there is more to water than the liquid that satisfies thirst or the ice that constitutes a snowflake. We know that there must be reasons why the sea has been compassed and why water has been bound.

One of the reasons perhaps is that somehow from the beginning and because of the limitations put upon the waters then, we are now consequently able to be alive; to be living and free, free to hope beyond hope, to hope beyond the rainbow, beyond the limitations put upon the waters, to hope beyond the difficulties that seem to surround us here on this wonder full earth.

And all this because - - -

". . .I cut out the place I had decreed for it and imposed gates and a bolt. 'Come so far,' I said, 'and no farther; here your proud waves must break!' "

Wine and Wineskins, Old and New

Christian scripture has a few "Do not's": Do not steal, Do not lie, Do not covet, Do not embarrass other people, and so on. Other religions have similar admonitions. The "Do's" also are important: Love God more than anybody else, Love your neighbor as yourself, Honor your parents, Behave yourself in public, Pray daily, Attend church, mosque, temple, or synagogue regularly, and so on.

We all know the reasons for the "Do's"—it simply makes no sense to do otherwise (although we find excuses when we fail to conform). We also know the reasons for all but one of the "Do not's"—the one that warns to not put new wine in old wineskins.

That is, we are told that if we put new wine into old wineskins they will burst. But why will they burst? The explanation illuminates our search for hope.

First of all, wineskins are made from leather that is made out of goatskins. Not lamb or sheepskins; they leak; whether filled with old or new wine, they leak.

Long ago, the man or woman who first successfully used the hide of an animal for any purpose (perhaps for protection against the cold— or maybe as a disguise to frighten an adversary) he or she rather quickly regretted their desire to improve their situation. Within a few hours after the animal was skinned (its hide was not tanned) it started to deteriorate in a decidedly odiferous manner.

One wonders how long it was, a week or two, or more likely several years, until our progenitors learned about tanning, the process that prevents the rapid deterioration of animal skins by converting the raw animal skin into leather.

Perhaps that first tanning resulted from a flood and some animals drowned in the rising water along with a few nearby downed and submerged oak trees. Some weeks later our progenitor happened along and noticed that the hides on the dead animals had changed. Further investigation (which may have required still more years) revealed the details: The hides had been tanned into leather by the tannin in the bark of the oak trees.

Almost all plants contain tannins. Oak bark, chestnut tree roots, and cashew nut hulls are especially rich in tannins. Chemically, tannins are known as "polyphenols." Polyphenols are a class of molecules with several attached hydrogen and oxygen atoms sort of sticking out, like porcupine quills, all over. In general, the hydrogen atoms are more positively charged and the oxygen atoms more negatively charged than the hydrogen and oxygen atoms in water molecules that we have previously described.

In any event, 2000 years ago the Hebrews and other peoples used oak bark and goatskins to make wineskins. Goatskins have three layers, the hairy epidermis layer on the outside, the corium, or *dermis*, a thick middle layer, and an inner fatty layer. Unless the hide is promptly dried after skinning, it deteriorates within a few hours. The epidermis and hair are readily separated from the rest of the hide at this time. The fatty layer is removed by scraping with a flat stone that has at least one sharp edge. The remainder, the corium, typically is as much as one-quarter inch thick and moderately flexible. It is fabricated into a bag and filled with water and shredded oak bark. In a week or less, the tanning process is finished.

The leather bag is emptied of the water and oak bark, rinsed and flushed, ready to receive new wine. Depending on the size of the goat, a typical wineskin holds from 50 to 100 pounds of wine.

The preceding chapter described how water molecules are held together as clusters by the mutually attractive positive and negative charges on the hydrogen and oxygen atoms of the constituent water molecules. The corium of all mammals, including your corium and mine, is principally composed of protein molecules and water molecules. There are thousands of different protein molecules and many of them have names; "collagen" is the name assigned to the kinds of protein molecules that comprise the major component in the corium of mammalian skins.

Collagen molecules are very long (long for a molecule, that is) and flexible. Think of a very long strand of spaghetti cooked to "*al dente*" with hydrogen, oxygen, and occasional nitrogen atoms forming the strand. (The other atoms in the strand are principally carbon but they are not pertinent to our story.) Next, think of several (a dozen or more) *al dente* spaghetti strands grouped together in parallel to form a bunch of strands, with a bit of tomato sauce (representing water) visible in between the strands.

As described in the preceding chapter, the hydrogen and oxygen atoms in this water are also attracted to the oxygen and hydrogen atoms of the collagen strands. That is, the sauce between the strands holds adjacent strands together by the negative/positive attraction thus resulting in bunches of flexible strands.

Consider several thousand or more of these bunches spread out into a layer that is several bunches wide and long and a few bunches thick, with more tomato sauce added to represent still more water. This is what the corium layer in your skin (and in goatskin too) would look like if we could magnify it several million times to make these details visible.

With all that water in it, the corium is susceptible to rapid deterioration by bacteria, fungi, and other nasty entities. If we could get rid of most of the water we would then render the corium resistant to this kind of attack. It would then become a durable, flexible, sturdy, tough and useful material.

To get rid of the water, we will use polyphenols; we will tan the hide.

Polyphenol molecules in the corium compete with water molecules. The water molecules in corium are in constant motion, wiggling, vibrating, jumping away from attachment, returning to where they were attached or to another empty spot recently vacated by a different water molecule. But in a polyphenol molecule the hydrogen atoms are more positively charged and oxygen atoms more negatively charged than in a water molecule.

Consequently, if a loose polyphenol molecule is nearby when a spot is vacated by a water molecule, the polyphenol molecule, with a stronger positive hydrogen and negative oxygen will claim the empty spot for itself. The bond now is stronger than it was with the water. Bonded polyphenol molecules also move around, but once they are attracted to a particular spot on a corium molecule, they tend to stay longer because the bond is stronger.

Eventually, with uncountable numbers of water and polyphenol molecule exchanges involved per second, it will not take too long before the corium is converted to leather with only a few millions of water molecules still present here and there in the tanned collagen-polyphenol product. A few million water molecules is not very many. A piece of leather with only that many water molecules is a piece of dry leather, no longer subject to rapid deterioration.

And now with tightly sewn seams that form our leather goatskin bag into a non-leaking wineskin, only one problem remains: the wine itself.

In ancient days, to make wine, you put crushed grapes into an amphora, a ceramic vessel with a curved but pointy bottom and a typical capacity of twenty to fifty gallons. In due course, spores of yeast from the air or already on the grape skins would begin their work forming themselves into cells of living yeast that, feasting on the sugar in the grape juice, produce carbon dioxide, ethyl alcohol, malic acid, flavoring agents, and other minor products.

The carbon dioxide bubbles off as a gas. Ethyl alcohol and various flavoring constituents, the desired products, remain along with the malic acid and the water from the juice. Some strains of yeast do better with the quantity of alcohol and the delectability of the flavoring components than other strains. It was a matter of chance back then whether you had yeast that produced a fine wine or a lesser quality. In any event, all yeasts produce some malic acid; and malic acid does not exactly enhance the flavor of wine.

Fortunately, back in those days the need for sterile conditions when making wine were not well understood. The bacteria present in the wine multiply at a slower rate than the yeast cells. Typically, by the time the new wine contains approximately 13 to 17 percent alcohol the yeast cells will mostly have drowned in their own alcohol and the bacteria will have just started to multiply.

As they multiply, the bacteria consume the malic acid and excrete carbon dioxide (which bubbles off) and lactic acid. A little lactic acid in wine enhances the flavor. So all in all, to have some bacteria in your wine turns out to be a lucky accident—except for one more thing.

In those days 2000 years ago wineskins were used to transport wines. There were no small one quart or so sized wineskins to stuff in one's hip pocket or carry in a sling for an occasional nip or two during the day. That simply was not done. Wine was used as a beverage at dinner, often diluted with an equal quantity of water. The trouble was that occasionally a filled wineskin would burst and the transporter, or whoever else owned that wine, was the loser. It didn't take long before a solution was devised: Do not put new wine into old, used, wineskins.

Why not? Remember that little bit of water that remained in the tanned leather? The polyphenol molecules are bigger and heavier, they do not evaporate. Water molecules in the leather slowly migrate to the surface of the leather and either enter the wine, or, if they migrate to the outside surface of the leather, evaporate into the air. Either way, the leather where the water was shrinks and becomes less pliable, you could even say kind of brittle.[16]

In plain English, an old wine skin has some shrunken, brittle spots and if you put 50 or more pounds of new wine into that wineskin and then propose to transport the filled wineskin on your camel or donkey over a road that is not a smooth paved superhighway, that filled wineskin is going to be subjected to at least a few rugged jostles and jolts along the way. It may not survive the trip. And neither will the wine.

Now we know the explanation.

But this story also has a moral and a precept.

The moral of this story is not that we now know the explanation for the "Do nots." The moral is that we already know, and have known for some time the reasons for the "Do's," and it is about time that we acted on this knowledge, each one of us, individually and jointly.

If we really truly while we are here want It To Be Better Than This, we already know, especially if we do pay attention to those "Do's," that it *will* become better.

---

[16] For the past 500 years (approximately) but not before that, tanned leather has been processed further in order to prevent brittleness as the leather ages.

And the precept?

Simply put, the precept with respect to new wine and old wineskins is obvious: Violate this precept and because of that violation you will cause a mess—spilled wine all over the place.

More to the point, violations of the precepts that govern the interactions between and among you and me and everybody also cause a mess, sometimes a big mess—even a catastrophe.

How so?

The answer involves love; it is complicated. I hope I can explain it clearly.

We humans are supposed to love God, our Creator. That is the big difference between us and animals and plants and bacteria and other similar things.

Some people confuse love with other emotions. When you love somebody you do what they ask you to do, even if it is difficult to do it. When they love you, they don't ask you to do impossible things. To love someone means that you do not do anything that they would not want you to do.

The other thing, the really most important thing about love, is that you do not have to do it. Nobody forces you to love. If somebody who loves you asks you to do something, even if it is easy to do, you do not have to do it. "Young man, tie your shoe." conveys an obligation to respond in love, not a requirement to comply.

Of course, failure to comply, failure to respond in love does carry a consequence. Rejecting the precept to tie your shoe could result in tripping and falling.

It is the same in more important matters. Some people aver that God is not a loving God because he allows earthquakes and floods and tornados and all sorts of catastrophes, even head-on collisions, and train wrecks, and murders, and plagues and other abominations. I agree, if that is what God is like, he surely is not a loving God. But that is not what God is like. I don't know Him very well yet but I do know two things for sure. He loves you and He loves me—each of us, equally. That is what fathers do.

We have all heard this false argument before. It was summarized long ago in the book of Wisdom[17]:

> "Our life is short and dreary, there is no remedy when our end comes, no one is known to have come back after they died. We came into being by chance and afterwards it will be as though we had never been. The breath in our nostrils is a puff of smoke, reason is merely a spark from the beating of our hearts. Extinguish these and the body turns to ashes, while the spirit melts away like the yielding air. In time, our name will be forgotten, nobody will remember what we have done. Our life will pass away like wisps of cloud, dissolving like the mist that the sun's rays drive away and its heat dispels. Our days are the passing of a shadow, our end is without return. The seal is affixed. No one comes back."

And the argument continues:

> "Come then, let us enjoy the good things of today. Let us use these things with the zest of youth. Take your fill of the dearest wines. Enjoy the flowers of spring. Crown yourselves with pleasures before they wither. Leave the signs of your revelry everywhere, this is our portion, this is our lot!"

To the contrary[18]:

God did not make Death. He takes no pleasure in destroying the living; he created all things to exist. The creatures of the world have Life, not Death, in them. God created human beings to exist forever. To be immortal, an image of his own nature.

---

[17] See Wisdom 2: 1-9.

[18] See Wisdom again, 1: 13-14 and 2: 23-25.

Death[19] came into the world through the Devil's envy, as those who belong to him find to their cost. So do not assist in causing death (those catastrophes—and all the other disasters) by the errors of your ways; don't invite these destructions through the work of your hands.

If we want to prevent that mess of spilled wine, if we wish to avoid tripping over a shoelace, we know how to make it happen. If we want to rid our earth of catastrophes and chaos, waste, woes, and worries, and all the others in between, we know how to make that happen too.

---

[19] And in addition to Death also came (in alphabetical order) Catastrophe, Chaos, Corrosion, Corruption, Damage, Decay, Decomposition, Depression, Destruction, Disaster, Discomfort, Disease, Disorder, Distress, Drought, Earthquake, Envy, Evil, Fire, Flood, Genocide, Grief, Harm, Hate, Havoc, Injury, Malaise, Mischief, Misery, Mold, Murder, Obliteration, Oblivion, Outrage, Pandemonium, Poison, Prejudice, Putrefaction, Riot, Ruin, Selfishness, Shame, Sin, Subversion, Tragedy, Tumult, Violence, War, Waste, Woe, Worry, to name a few.

It Can Become Known

Consider the flames from wood burning in a fireplace or a campfire. The dancing patterns disclose ever changing, fascinating designs. In an instant what is seen, what was real, is there no longer. Seen once, the evanescent pattern will not be seen again.

Look more closely. When wood is heated it changes. It forms vapors of other substances: methyl alcohol (also called wood alcohol), acetic acid (the sour component of vinegar), acetone (a common component of fingernail polish remover), and other vapors and gases including hydrogen, methane, acetylene, and carbon monoxide.

The yellow flames we see are the colored light from burning particles of carbon. These particles are quite small, smaller even than the particles of the flour used in cooking. When these particles burn they emit yellow light. When larger carbon particles burn, the color of the light is yellow tinged with red. Try it!

Like this: Make some burnt toast (nicely black, please). The black toast is mostly carbon. Put some of the black toast on a sheet of paper and crush the chunks into smaller pieces with the bowl of a spoon. When some of the crushed particles are more or less about the size of particles of flour, take a pinch between thumb and fingers and let the black powder drop into the flame of a burning candle. Notice that the yellow of microscopically small carbon particles burning in a flame is, in the sprinkle of larger carbon particles, tinged with red.

If you wish, use flour instead. Put a small amount of flour (about a quarter teaspoon) on a sheet of paper. Then with care, blow the flour off the paper and into the flame. In the heat of the fire, the flour particles are quickly toasted into black carbon particles with the same red and yellow colored sparkles as a result.

Listen to wood that is burning. You can hear the soft hiss of the vapors and gases issuing from the wood. If you look carefully, especially at a new log that has just been put into the fire, you can see that flames seem to spurt from the surface of the blazing wood. Look more closely; in the small space between the base of a spurting flame and the surface of the wood, there is no flame at all. In the space where you see no flame, the invisible vapors and gases, formed under pressure within the wood, hiss as they come forth, mixing with the air as they do so. Then, under the influence of the heat from the surrounding flames, and now mixed with a sufficient quantity of oxygen from the air, the spurting vapors and gases burst into flame.

Look again at the base of a spurting flame; you will see that the portion of the flame at the bottom, next to the space where there is no flame, is blue in color. The particles of carbon are not yet hot enough to burn. And other portions of the flame, further from the bottom, are other colored—orange and pale red.

The gases and vapors spurting from the heated wood (methyl alcohol, acetic acid, acetone, hydrogen, methane, acetylene, carbon monoxide etc.) emit the blue, orange, and pale red colors as they partially burn forming water vapor, carbon dioxide, and the very small carbon particles that will then immediately also burn forming the yellow colored dancing flames.

You can see the same effects in a candle flame. Most people think that a candle flame is yellow. But we now know better. Look carefully at the flame of a burning candle. It is not all yellow; look carefully, you can see other colors.

Next, consider a thunderstorm. A lot of noise, several flashes of lightning, more than a few bushels of rain, all accompanied by windy conditions. What else?

To find out what else there is for thunderstorms, we could check into some reference works; an encyclopedia, even Wikipedia maybe; or ask a meteorological friend.

Of course there is the question, "Why bother?" After all we could probably continue to live as productive a life as we are now achieving without knowing any more about thunderstorms than that they consist of a lot of noise, lightning, rain, and wind.

OK, instead of thunderstorms, how about Mozart's 39ᵗʰ? Or a bit closer yet to concerns that really matter: What about my interactions with others?

In the earlier part of this discussion I demonstrated that from an increase in the intensity of our observation, we can learn more about a physical phenomenon. As an old retired scientist, I enjoy the adventure involved when I increase the intensity of observations of a phenomenon. Of course, what is important here is not my delight, rather, it is your satisfaction.

The principle is straightforward:

Most of what is unknown about a physical phenomenon can become known. And in some instances all that is currently unknown about a physical phenomenon will become known.

Therefore, it could be correct to conclude that to some degree what is now unknown concerning a non-physical phenomenon can become known. Example: How many angels can be on the head of a pin before putting the next one on would force one of the earlier occupants to fall off?

In pondering this question, I have concluded that angels, being non-physical, are not subject to gravitational attraction and therefore none would fall off. (What would happen I do not know. I suspect that, angels being non-physical, you cannot get them onto the head of a pin in the first place.)

More important questions include: Who is Jesus Christ? Was he both human and divine? What was his purpose? What is your purpose in life? How might you be better satisfied with the way you are fulfilling that purpose? Who is God anyway? Does he love each of us as much as some people say he does? If he loves each of us so much, why does he allow earthquakes and tornadoes and floods? Or is it all a big flat joke of some kind?

I submit that it is a long way from a joke. He does love us; more than anything He loves us. Maybe he wants to help us reflect the love he has for us by pointing out to us that we too love other people, people that we don't even know. For example, when there is a big earthquake somewhere many of us make a small or bigger sacrifice and donate money or goods to the earthquake relief organization.

Could that be maybe the reason there are big earthquakes every once in a while? When a friend encounters some kind of misfortune, what do you do? Could it be that maybe one of the reasons they had such a problem was to help us more responsibly recognize our love for our friend?

God does love us, but he is not going to force anybody to love him in return. Is it possible then that he is willing to trick us into loving others more so that maybe we will figure out that it is a good idea, considering what love is, to also love him more, now that we are increasing our love for our friend and for those unknown earthquake victims?

You want proof? You would like to be sure of this love business? You would like to know how it is that if he loves us so much he also allows earthquakes and tornadoes and floods and horrible accidents and wars and people who torture other people and all the rest of these kinds of things?

I have already explained to you how to know that. Of course it is not proof; and considering what love is, proof is not necessary—nor is it possible. Either you know it or you do not know it. Take your pick.

Transfiguration

White is the presence of color, all the colors. All the colors of the rainbow, that is: red, orange, yellow, green, blue, indigo, violet[20]. Light that is called "white light" is composed of all the colors of the rainbow. It is reasonable to conjecture that Joseph's coat of many colors as described in scripture was made of rainbow colored fabric— in effect of all the colors that, together, comprise white—the presence of all the colors. In this chapter I suggest that it is also reasonable to conjecture that white, consisting of all the colors, has an entirely different significance.

Are there any other colors? Yes, purple for example; a mixture of red and indigo, is a color not found in rainbows. On the other hand, other color-mixtures, red-orange, yellow-green, pink, blue-green, and other similar color combinations are in rainbows. Rainbows contain all the colors that are visible to the human eye except purple.

White is a mixture of all the colors of light that are in the rainbow[21].

Are there any other colors that we can see besides purple and the colors of the rainbow? Yes, but not with our eyes. We can feel the heat from a hot iron or a steam-filled radiator. That "color" is called infrared. We can tan our skin (or if we are too eager, get sun-burned) by light that is ultraviolet colored. Some insects, for example bees and various other pollinating insects, can see the colors of infrared

---

[20] Today, the colors indigo and violet are commonly called "deep blue" and "very deep blue," or equivalent phrases.

[21] When the seven rainbow colors of paint (pigment) are mixed, the resulting mixture is dark gray or black. Various colors of light also can be mixed, for example, by using several slide projectors, each projecting a different color, all onto the same screen. The result on the screen is white when all seven rainbow colors, red, orange, yellow, green, blue, indigo, and violet are projected on the same screen.

and ultraviolet light with their eyes. With the help of a radio or cell phone we can detect still other colors. On a colored TV screen we can see the visible colors generated by invisible (to humans) photons emitted from the antenna of a TV broadcasting station or satellite. Similarly, the antenna of a radio station emits colored light that your radio detects and converts into sound that you hear.

These remarks require an explanation. The explanation will regrettably but necessarily be complicated and technical. I guarantee that it will not be painful, but it will require your full-concentrated-attention.

All light consists of photons. Photons are particles that have energy that we can measure as frequency (as though the particles were vibrating). All photons move very fast, 186,000 miles per second in the vacuum of space, and somewhat slower through liquids and solids. You can think of photons as projectiles emitted from the sun, from a hot iron, from a steam-filled radiator, from a radio or TV broadcasting antenna, from a light bulb or fluorescent bulb in the lamp stand that you turned on in order to read this sentence. Some of those photons bounced off of the page, passed through the lens of your eyes, and were absorbed by the retina of your eyes, generating nerve impulses that enabled you to read this sentence.

Photons that have frequencies greater than those from a TV or radio broadcasting antenna but less than photons which can be detected by the human eye are emitted from hot objects—your cup of coffee, a radiator filled with steam that heats your home or apartment on a cool day, or the hot iron used to remove the wrinkles in a laundered garment. These photons are called "infrared" photons. See Figure 3.

Ultraviolet photons are emitted by the sun and from earth-bound so-called "tanning" devices. These photons have a higher frequency than those that are visible to the human eye. UV-A photons have less energy, a lesser frequency, than UV-B photons, as might be expected, since UV-B radiation is more harmful than UV-A radiation.

The photons from an X-Ray device have even greater energy, greater frequency that is, than UV-B photons. As you know, X-Ray photons can penetrate through human tissues, through softer tissue more readily, and with lesser ease through dense tissue, such as bones.

Gamma ray photons are generated in the radioactive decay of unstable atomic nuclei. They have still more energy, a greater frequency, passing readily through human tissue, for example, and causing damage as they do so.

When stars explode the debris is scattered in all directions. Some of that debris is photons, called "Cosmic ray photons". These photons pass through the earth's orbit continuously. Cosmic ray photons have the highest energy of all photons. Fortunately, the approximately 100 mile thick blanket of air surrounding the earth is sufficient to prevent cosmic ray photons from adversely affecting earth-bound life processes. Astronauts need shields of various sorts to protect themselves against the harm caused by cosmic ray photons and other cosmic ray debris. Photons of intermediate energy generate the colors we can see. For example, photons that the normal human eye sees as red have frequencies (oscillations) between 380,000,000,000,000 and 490,000,000,000,000 each second[22]. As shown in Figure 3, photons that the normal human eye sees as violet (very deep blue) have frequencies between 690,000,000,000,000 and 830,000,000,000,000 Hertz.

It is somewhat mildly interesting to note that for the eye, the range of visible photon frequencies approximately one octave whereas for the ear, the range of audible air vibration frequencies is approximately 20 to 20,000 Hertz[23], a range of almost ten octaves. The following is even more interesting:

The problem faced by the writers of the three synoptic gospels in their account of Christ's transfiguration was how to describe the whiteness of his garment. Mark tried, using the Greek, *lian*, meaning "much, very, exceedingly." Matthew similarly, with *phos* signifying the "opposite of darkness." And Luke also, he chose *ex-astrapt* that means "to send forth lightning, to flash out, to shine, to be radiant."

---

[22] In Figure 3, the designations such as 10^4 Hz, 10^8 Hz, 10^{20} Hz, and so on, represent frequencies--oscillations per second. The exponents, 4, 8, 20, and so on, are decimal point or zero "counters"; thus: exponent 4, 4 zeros, 10,000, exponent 20, 20 zeros, 100,000,000,000,000,000,000. Frequencies are called "Hertz" (abbreviated as 'Hz').

Thus, 10^4 Hz, 10^8 Hz, 10^{20} Hz, represent 10,000 oscillations per second, 100,000,000 oscillations per second, and 100,000,000,000,000,000,000 oscillations per second, respectively.

[23] Vibrations per second, for sound waves.

The synoptic authors certainly did the best they could but their problem was that there is no word, in any human language, for the white of Christ's garment.

How can this be, no word for the color of a white garment? White is white, that is obvious, is it not?

No it is not obvious. Figure 3 is a diagram. It shows *all* the colors, those that are visible to the human eye, and those that are not. White is the name we give to all the colors, taken as a whole, that we can see in the rainbow.

Taken as a whole, *all* the colors represented in Figure 3, if we could see them, would be seen as &^%<u>w h i t e</u>%^&, a color that you and I have never seen and therefore have no word to describe it. That &^%<u>w h i t e</u>%^& is indescribable.

Until they went up on that mountain with Christ, Peter, James, and John had never seen such a white as that either, and they had no word to describe it after they saw it. How they did describe it when they finally could speak of their experience, what words they did use, we do not know. What we do know is that by the time it was written down by Mark, Matthew, and Luke, they too had trouble—there was still no word to describe the color of that garment. There still is not.

If we could see it today its whiteness would be so intense as to defy description in any of the words that we humans have at our disposal. Without the word I need, I can only try to explain the color of Christ's garment:

Figure 3 is not what it seems to be, a diagram on a printed page approximately an inch wide and a bit more than five or six inches long. Actually, it should be shown as a diagram about an inch wide but long enough to more than fill the pages of all the books that will ever be published in the history of the world—more than thousands of miles long, that is. How so? Look at the top half-inch of the diagram, the space between 0 Hz and 10^2 Hz. That space represents 100 Hz (from 0 to 10^2 Hz). But the next half inch, from 10^2 Hz to 10^4 Hz, represents 9,900 Hz (from 100 to 10000 Hz). If that second space were printed at the same scale as the first half inch (100 Hz in half an inch), it would be 99 half-inches (49 inches plus one-half inch) long.

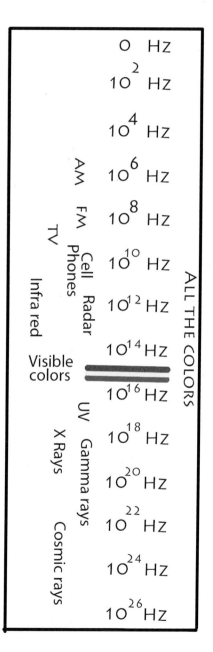

Fig. 3 - The Photon Spectrum, also known as the Electro-magnetic Spectrum.

Similarly, the third half inch of Figure 3 comprises 990,000 Hz. At a scale of one-half inch for each 100 Hz it would need 4950 inches (412.5 feet) for the third interval. The fourth interval requires 495,000 inches (7.8 miles), and the fifth still more yet.

Actually, in Figure 3 as we proceed down the diagram, the corrected scale length becomes larger and larger; starting at a half-inch, the next interval is 49½ inches, and the next interval is 412.5 feet, then the next is 7.8 miles. Continuing downward, the scale increases rapidly and the bottommost (last) half-inch of Figure 3, from 10^{24} Hz to 10^{26} Hz, is 7,900,000,000,000,000,000 miles long.

For comparison, consider the star Arcturus (astronomers call it Alpha Boötis, which means "Bear guard"). Arcturus is the star "guarding" the tail of Ursa Major, the Great Bear constellation. Approximately, Arcturus is 235,000,000,000,000 miles from earth. But 7,900,000,000,000,000,000 miles is more than thirty thousand times longer than the distance from here to Alpha Boötis. Figure 1, representing all the colors is very long indeed. That is a lot of colors.

Joseph's garment was a coat of only the visible colors, the colors of the rainbow.	Christ's garment is a coat of all the colors, the colors of the photon spectrum.
Through his coat of many colors, Joseph presaged his captivity and later, his prestige in Egypt by which he achieved the rescue of his people from starvation, providing for them the gift of sustenance.	Christ's garment is a coat of all the colors. He is able to save his people with salvation.

Twelve Stones and Miracles

We will get to Stones later, and we will save Miracles until the end. But now to start with consider the created Universe, the whole shebang. What is it made of?

As far as we know, the Universe is made of a variety of corporealities. Some of them are: *Dark Matter*—we don't know much about what it really is; and maybe there are *Gravitons*—maybe not, but if so they probably are particles of some sort that are responsible for gravity; also *Neutrinos*—very tiny little things in continuous motion that travel very fast in straight lines and can penetrate anything, leaving a mere trace of their passage; plus *Cosmic Rays*—particles of various sorts that travel very fast and penetrate other stuff often causing lots of damage; and *Photons*—particles of light that comprise the electromagnetic spectrum; and, finally:

Physical Matter—the wood and rocks and people and air and buildings and everything else that we can see and feel and touch including our arms and legs and brains and livers and all the rest of what everything is made of.

All physical matter is composed of one or more elements. Currently, there are 118 known elements of which 28 are artificial. All of this earth is made from the remaining 90 elements[24].

The familiar and unfamiliar names of some of those 90 elements, as we already know, are: praseodymium, iron, copper, astatine, ruthenium, silver, gold, osmium, aluminum, cesium, germanium, and so on. All the atoms of an element have the same number of protons in their nuclei.

---

[24] The Periodic Table shows 114 elements including 24 artificial elements. The missing artificial elements are elements numbered 113, 115, 117, and 118 (temporarily) named "Ununtrium", "Ununpentium", "Ununseptium" and "Ununoctium", respectively. Also, element number 112, Ununbium, is now named "Copernicium" honoring Copernicus, the 16th century Polish astronomer.

Other elements have a different number of protons, each element a unique number of protons. For example, hydrogen (symbol H) has 1 proton in the nucleus; for iron (symbol Fe) there are 26 protons in each nucleus of iron atoms. See numbers 1 and 26 in the Periodic Table described below.

To continue: Visualize an atom as a very small sphere with an even smaller nucleus in the center. The nucleus is composed of one or more positively charged protons ("positively charged" is an abstract term) and neutrons that have no charge. Surrounding the nucleus of an atom are one or more electrons. Electrons are negatively charged (abstract term). In an atom of an element the number of electrons is the same as the number of protons in the nucleus–just enough to balance the positive charge of the nucleus—so that the atom is neutral, neither positively or negatively charged. There is more, but this much information will do for now.

Until the middle of the nineteenth century the inter-relationships between and among the elements that constitute physical matter were not well understood. Scientists suspected, but did not fully recognize, the existence of inter-relationships. Then in the 1870s there was a revolution in our understanding of these relationships. It is called the "Periodic Table". It was conceived by Dmitry Mendeleev[25], a Russian chemistry professor while he was writing a textbook, the "Principles of Chemistry". In the Periodic Table, elements with similar properties are grouped in vertical columns. Horizontally, the interactions of each vertical grouping with electrons increases in strength from left to right.

See Figure 4, the Periodic Table. It shows 114 elements including 24 artificial elements and the 90 natural elements. Each block shows the symbol of an element and, in the upper left corner of the block, a number. That number is the "atomic number," the number of electrons in each of the neutral atoms of that element as well as the number of protons in the nucleus of that element. Look at the number 20 (left side, just below the upper left corner). Each neutral calcium atom has 20 electrons. Consider fluorine, number 9 (upper right corner). Each neutral fluorine atom has 9 electrons.

---

[25] The 17th child in a family of 17 children.

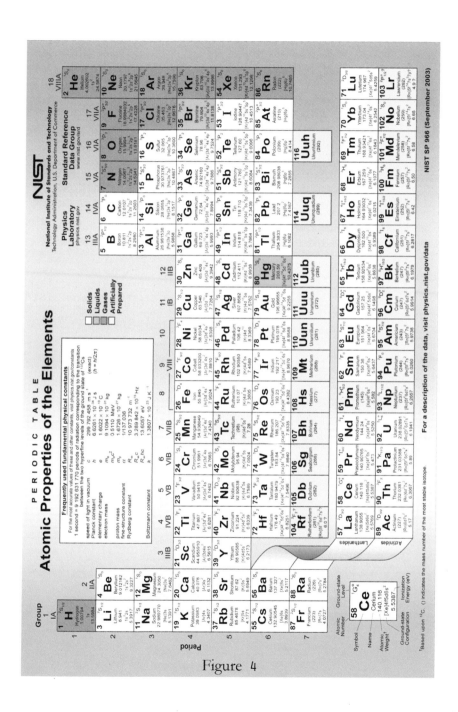

Figure 4

Atoms of an element can combine with other atoms of the same element. For example, two oxygen atoms form the oxygen molecules present in the air we breathe; two nitrogen atoms similarly produce the nitrogen molecules. Copper atoms in the millions of billions join, thus forming copper metal. Gold and silver, iron—all the other metals--similarly combine.

Atoms combine with atoms by sharing electrons. The sharing can be equal: two chlorine atoms share two electrons forming a molecule of chlorine, Cl_2. In water the oxygen-hydrogen bonds, a pair of electrons, the sharing is unequal, favoring oxygen, which gives it a small negative charge thereby producing a small positive charge on each of the two hydrogens, H_2O.

Ethyl alcohol is a compound with two atoms of carbon, six atoms of hydrogen, and one atom of oxygen. In ethyl alcohol the atoms of carbon have four electrons (out of the six, total) that they are "willing" to share; the six hydrogen atoms have one electron but they are willing to share that one, an oxygen atom out of its eight electrons is willing to share two electrons.

The result, Figure 5, is interesting.

Figure 5. A two-dimensional representation of an ethyl alcohol molecule; each dashed line represents a pair of shared electrons.

Here in the bond between the two carbon atoms the electron pair sharing is equal, unequal between the carbons and hydrogens causing the hydrogens to be very slightly positive, unequal between the carbon and oxygen causing the carbon to be slightly positive. And (as with water) the bond between the hydrogen and oxygen involves unequal sharing causing the hydrogen to have a small positive charge and the oxygen a small negative charge.

Consider calcium fluoride, CaF_2. (The geological name for calcium fluoride is "Fluorite.") Fluorine, atomic number 9 (upper right corner) is a unique element. Of all the known elements fluorine does not readily share any of its electrons with other atoms when it forms compounds. Fluorine is an impatient element, it takes electrons from other atoms; it does not patiently wait for an electron to be donated. With calcium, for example, a fluorine atom simply takes one of the electrons from a calcium atom and then another fluorine atom takes yet another electron from the same calcium atom to form calcium fluoride.

If you apply sufficient energy, such as a surge of high ampere current to a compound of fluorine, say calcium fluoride, the fluorine atoms will be forced off of the calcium atoms. They will form fluorine molecules, F_2. Fluorine molecules are very reactive; they tend to take electrons from any handy molecules that happen to be nearby. If water molecules happen to be nearby, the water is destroyed. To the human observer, the water appears to be burning in an exceedingly hot fire.

Now we can get to the Stones and Miracles.

Limestone is a form of rock found all over the world; and fluorite, CaF_2, is commonly found in limestone deposits. Commercially useful accumulations of fluorite, for example, are found in the limestone deposits located in southern Illinois and adjacent areas in Kentucky. In most other locations the fluorite in the limestone, although commonly present, is not as abundant.

Now for our story we go to Haifa, Israel. Today, Mount Carmel, a 1500 foot high limestone hill, is located within the city of Haifa. It is a scenic spot; westward from the top of Mount Carmel the view of the Mediterranean Sea is memorable.

Centuries ago Mount Carmel was in the boonies, sort of alone on the Eastern coast of the Mediterranean Sea. As it is today, it was then a beautiful place with a great view of the sea; a fine spot to build an altar or two. And that is what Elijah and the priests of Baal did, a long time ago[26].

The idea was to find out whose deity was stronger, by testing to see which deity would ignite a sacrificial fire on their altar. The priests of

[26] 1 Kings: 21-39

Baal went first, imploring their god to bring down fire and ignite the wood and sacrificial bull on the altar that they had built. As you may recall, those priests implored very dramatically, even to the point of sticking themselves with swords and bleeding all over the place. But nothing happened.

Then Elijah built an altar using twelve large pieces of limestone that were handy nearby. He put wood on the altar and on top of the wood he put the butchered pieces of the sacrificial bull. Then he doused everything thoroughly with hundreds (more or less) of gallons of water, and after that he asked God to set fire to the sacrifice on his altar, and whammo! It happened. The fire consumed the wet wood and the bull and evaporated all the excess water.

From what I have already told you, you have probably, and correctly, guessed that fluorine was involved. The fluorine reacted with the water, causing it to appear to burn fiercely and drying all the wood which caught fire from the heat that was generated by the reaction of that fluorine with the water.

Where did the fluorine come from? From the fluorite in the limestone of the rocks that Elijah used to build his altar. How did the fluorine get loose from the fluorite? My guess is that a powerful bolt of cosmic rays caused the fluorite in the limestone rocks of the altar to release the fluorine from that fluorite. But of course that is necessarily an assumption.

The more important question is whether or not I have explained how the miracle happened. The answer is of course not. Perhaps I have accounted for some aspects of the miracle but there still remain several unaccounted-for details.

What is a miracle anyway?

A miracle is an event which requires the eye of faith to be recognized as a miracle.

> The acorn that becomes an oak tree.
> The origin of life for a child in the womb.
> The love we bear for others.
> The greatest miracle of all?

TRANSUBSTANTIATION !

The host changes yet remains the same. It is still nutritious, still digestible. But it is no longer plain bread. Now it is the Bread of Life, itself alive, living, the Body of Christ, the man who was also God and who suffered and died for us and who was resurrected on the third day. The wine, it still tastes exactly like wine; if you analyzed it, you would find that it is composed of ethyl alcohol, water, and a mixture of other substances that comprise its odor, flavor, and taste. But now it is not wine, it is the blood of Christ shed for us so that we might, one day, know indeed that it is better than it is now.

Changed but not changed.

How can this be?

By analogy, consider your shadow, It also changes yet remains the same. On a cloudy day, it is barely discernible. On a sunny day at noon, it is short but toward late afternoon and evening, it lengthens. While you twist or turn, your shadow changes.

But always it is your shadow:

Changing but remaining the same—unchanged.

The eye of faith, remember?

Being With

Consider two people in love. They can be with each other sitting in different chairs or on the same sofa, not speaking but communicating nevertheless, in love.

When you are in love it is possible to communicate without speaking.

One is silent when contemplating a beautiful flower. Think of a fine sunset, a redwood forest, a magnificent horse, a fine work of art, the dog or cat you had as a child, a poem, a glass of beer in the shade on a hot summer day (especially if you have been working where there was no shade). None of these spoke in words, but you and they did communicate.

Plants also communicate without words. When sagebrush plants are attacked by insects, the sagebrush emits an odiferous vapor. That vapor causes a nearby tomato plant to emit a different odiferous vapor—one that repels insects that otherwise would tend to attack tomato plants.

Bees and wasps communicate with us, rather effectively and without words, when we appear to them as having invaded their territory. Bees communicate with other bees from the same hive. Ants too— you have often seen ants scurrying about. Sometimes when meeting one another two ants will touch antennae for a moment or two and then, seemingly as a consequence, one of the two will scurry off in a direction different from its prior path--as though it had received instructions from the other ant.

Our sun and this earth also communicate without words. We can see the result. In the northern hemisphere it is called Aurora Borealis and in the southern hemisphere, Aurora Australis. These displays are caused by interacting magnetic fields coming from the earth and from the sun. Earth and sun communicating.

To explain, the core of this earth is an approximate sphere of hot molten iron alloy, approximately 4400 miles in diameter with an inner, solid core approximately 2200 miles in diameter. The molten iron alloy is in constant motion. That motion generates a magnetic field that extends several thousands of miles into space. We use this field when we use a compass to determine our direction. The stars, our sun included, use other methods to generate much stronger magnetic fields extending millions of miles into space. It is when the magnetic field from the sun interacts with the field from the earth that we see the Aurora Borealis or the Aurora Australis.

Compared to the stars, the magnetic field of the earth is definitely on the wimpy side. Even so, the northern and southern lights are magnificent. But when the magnetic fields from two stars interact and the two stars communicate with one another that must be some conversation!

As with two people in love, words are not needed. Being with suffices. We too can be with the One who loves us and we Him. Words are not needed. That too can be a real conversation.

Resurrection

"The whole universe is mysterious to me[27]."

This chapter is about the universe. It involves large numbers, numbers with several zeros, numbers so large that it is not possible to imagine how large these numbers are. Indeed, the universe is mysterious.

We already know about a few of the ninety elements that comprise the substance of the earth, including us—our arms and legs and livers and hair and all the rest of each of us. Now we can take a broader view and look at the whole universe.

About thirteen or fourteen billion years ago there was nothing that science, had it existed then, could detect. There was, for example, no time. There was no thing.

Then the universe began. It started with a big explosion of an exceedingly tiny particle. The entire physical universe to be was "in" this very small, microscopic, particle. There was no other place to be; no thing was anywhere else[28] because there was no such thing as another place in which any thing could be. This single tiny particle was all there was.

THEN IT EXPLODED!

A few seconds later the universe began to form; it was composed of protons, electrons, neutrons and neutrinos. One hundred seconds later, approximately ten percent of the protons and neutrons formed into helium nuclei: two protons and two neutrons in each atomic

---

[27] Amanda Winfield in Act 2 of The Glass Menagerie by Tennessee Williams

[28] There was only God, a triune spirit, and perhaps angels, also spirits. Spirits do not need a place to be "in".

nucleus. Electrons, also present, danced around always within the small space that was then the universe. At that time there were no atoms, although electrons were present, the universe was too hot for the electrons to be able to join with the nuclei and form helium atoms.

When the ten percent of the protons and neutrons formed the helium nuclei a great deal of energy in the form of photons, that is, light, was released. Until then, the universe had been dark, no light. Even today, some of those first photons are still present; in fact, they were first detected only a few years ago and it was that detection which is the basis of the "Big Bang" theory we are discussing in this chapter.

In the thirteen or fourteen billion years since then, the Universe today is still being formed. Today, in addition to dark matter, cosmic rays, photons, maybe gravitons and all the rest, the universe is composed of, approximately, (Here is our big number, too large to imagine how large it really is. It has to be printed in smaller type to get it all on a single line):

100,000,000,000,000,000,000,000,000,000,000,000,000,000,000, 000,000,000,000,000,000,000,000,000,000,000.[29] atoms.

Of the total, approximately 92 percent are hydrogen atoms, approximately 8 percent are helium atoms, and 0.001 percent, approximately, are all the other 88 natural atoms, carbon, oxygen, iron, copper, praseodymium, manganese, and so on.

The question is: Where did these other 88 elements come from? And the answer is:

FROM THE LIVING STARS.

How can you tell if something is alive? If it is born, if it grows, if it reproduces, if it communicates, if it dies, then it is (was) alive. Cancer cells do this. Bacteria do this. Plants do this. And insects and cows and horses and dogs and cats and other animals also. You and I too do this—and we also resurrect. And the stars do too.

---

[29] 10^{80}.(ten to the "eightieth")

The stars are alive? Yes, like us they are born, they grow, they (use magnetic fields to) communicate, they die, they reproduce after they resurrect, using the debris left over from the dead stars.

Pay attention; this gets a little complicated. About 100,000 years after the beginning, the universe had cooled down a little. The helium nuclei and electrons became helium atoms. Instead of dancing around all over the universe, many of the electrons, two for each helium nucleus, were attracted to the helium nuclei whereupon the helium nuclei became helium atoms. And the same thing happened to the protons, the hydrogen nuclei. One electron for each proton and bingo, we now have hydrogen atoms.

This is the picture of the universe then, about 100,000 years after the beginning: A large number of hydrogen and helium atoms, more than anyone could count or even imagine, swirling about, some moving fast, some slow, bumping into each other, mostly bouncing away after a collision, but once in a while staying together, held each to the other by gravity—a "twosome." And once in a while, a third atom, maybe hydrogen, or maybe helium, collides with an already joined pair and instead of bouncing away, stays with the other two, held by gravity, and now we have a threesome. Thousands, millions, billions, still more yet, threesomes were formed. And foursomes, fivesomes, six, seven, ten, twenty, seventy-fivesomes, and still growing (all this required hundreds of years) one-hundred-and-fiftysomes. And more yet. Thousandsomes, millionsomes, trillionsomes. Bigger and bigger and bigger, too-many-to-countsomes were formed. Thousands of years.

A star is born. More stars. **THE FIRST STARS.**

Each one mostly hydrogen, about 99%, with about 1% helium atoms.

Each star was:

Hot. Very hot. Hotter yet in the center. Heavy. Very heavy. Big gravitational force, especially in the center. Crowded. Very crowded in the center. Hydrogen nuclei get pushed together. Really pushed, pushed hard—all that gravity. Four hydrogen nuclei, that is, four protons, become two protons and two neutrons and form one helium nucleus. Again and again and again and . . . . .

Nuclear fusion! One helium nucleus weighs less than four hydrogen nuclei. Loss of mass means "Release of energy."

$E = mc^2$, remember?[30]

ENERGY IS RELEASED. STARLIGHT, STARBRIGHT.

Eventually, after millions of years, almost all of the hydrogen nuclei in a star will have been converted to helium nuclei. That star cools and shrinks. Then the helium nuclei become crowded, very crowded. Three helium nuclei become one carbon nucleus. Nuclear fusion again! One carbon nucleus weighs less than three helium nuclei.

Once again, $E = mc^2$, lots of energy appears and the star glows once more.

And when the helium is depleted the star collapses. If it was a small star to start with, it becomes a "White dwarf" star. If it was a big star, it explodes; in a telescope the explosion can be seen as a very bright light—a supernova. And in the explosion the helium nuclei and the carbon nuclei get knocked together in all sorts of ways. Out of the confusion other nuclei are formed: sulfur, oxygen, nitrogen, phosphorus, tin, iron, uranium, chlorine, copper, and so on. And when there are several supernovae; new element nuclei are scattered all over the place:

STARDUST.

Remember those

100,000,000,000,000,000,000,000,000,000,000,000,000,000, 000,000,000,000,000,000,000,000,000,000 1% helium and 99% hydrogen atoms? Most of them sort of stood around and watched while those first stars were born, lived, and died. And now for some of them it is their turn to do likewise.

---

[30] By analogy, suppose you had a sack with four oranges in it weighing one pound each. Then, still supposing, the next day the sack contained only one grapefruit which weighed three pounds. That sack would also be glowing with a bright, hot, light. In the cosmos when there is a loss of mass, energy is released as heat and light, E, and is equal to the mass that has been lost, m, multiplied by the square (the exponent 2) of the speed of light, c. The speed of light, 186,000 miles per second, squared, is a big number, 34,596,000,000, so when it is multiplied by the mass that has been lost the result (the energy that is released) is a very big number indeed.

THE SECOND GENERATION OF STARS.

But with a difference. This time, as some of the hydrogen and helium atoms condense and form new stars, they also, by gravitational attraction, collect many of the new atoms that were generated by the first supernovae--the sulfur, oxygen, nitrogen, phosphorus, tin, iron, uranium, chlorine, copper, and other elements. When the larger stars of this second generation die as supernova still more atoms of sulfur, oxygen, . . . uranium, chlorine, copper, et cetera, more new elements, are formed in those supernova explosions:

MORE STARDUST.

In the thirteen or fourteen billion years since the beginning there has been enough time for one more generation of stars and, as they die, their supernovae make more of the elements, the stardust, the elements that comprise our physical bodies—yours, mine, everyone's.

YOU, ME, EVERYBODY, EACH ONE OF US, ARE RESURRECTED FROM THE STARS.

This is what happens to stars[31] when they are resurrected: Some of their stardust becomes included in new-born stars and some becomes planets, such as our earth. Our bodies are made from the elements in the earth. We are resurrected, living stars.

The resurrection of stars to form new stars involves events that are unimaginable. *We also are resurrected stars* and this resurrection has an unimaginable aspect.

We too will be resurrected; and by analogy therefore *it is not possible to imagine* what it will be like when we are resurrected.

BUT SURELY IT WILL BE BETTER THAN IT IS NOW.

---

[31] Thomas Merton was right when he wrote that each of us is walking around "shining like the sun". "Confessions of a Guilty Bystander," Doubleday, 1966.

Jumping

Some years ago each one of us was in our mother's womb. We started as fertilized eggs, zygotes, and as we grew and developed we became embryos and three months later, fetuses. About six months after that we became new-born babies after living in a nice, safe, warm and moist enclosure for a total of approximately nine months.

However, this is not to imply that in the womb we were ignorant of our surroundings; in fact we responded to them. Those of us who have been pregnant have described, perhaps while pregnant, to those of us who cannot become pregnant evidence that a fetus is aware of its surroundings. For example, at three to four months, the child in the womb becomes sufficiently vigorous so that its kicking and squirming can be felt by the mother. And as the child grows if the mother massages the spot where she feels the movement, the child often will move its foot or hand toward the mother's hand in response.

Many mothers report that at about six months, the child in the womb moves as though it is keeping time with music the mother hears on the radio or TV. Not too long after that, or even sooner, as the child grows and becomes stronger, the kicking and squirming can become painful at times.

It is necessary now to change the subject. As a growing child, say about two or three years old, we probably did a bit of jumping. We jumped on all sorts of occasions. As adults we can observe the jumping child. They jump to get over an object. They jump rope. They often jump when they try to catch a ball. When startled, even you and I will usually jump a bit and so will the small child.

However, when jumping for joy, the jump is different; it is distinguishable. Probably more than for any other reason, the small child will jump for the pure joy of jumping. When a child jumps for joy, you can tell the difference; you can readily see that it is jumping for joy.

As far as we know, however, only one child in the history of the human race jumped for joy while still in the womb.[32] His name (after he was born about three months later) was John. As an adult he became known as John the Baptist. He jumped for joy in the womb—his mother Elizabeth said so—when he heard his cousin Mary's voice greeting his mother. Mary was pregnant with Jesus at the time—as you perhaps recall—and she had come to Elizabeth's home to help her in her old age because she was pregnant with John the Baptist.

The first question is how did Elizabeth know that her child was jumping for joy and not simply squirming when he heard Mary's voice?

Jumping for joy is distinguishable from other kinds of jumping. Elizabeth may have been an old woman when she was carrying John in her womb, but she certainly knew that the child in her womb had been moving around for the past several weeks. As an old woman who thought she would never become pregnant, she probably was particularly fond of the small children in her neighborhood and enjoyed watching them at play. From those observations it is reasonable to conclude that Elizabeth knew very well the unique characteristics of joy-jumping children. So when John jumped upon hearing Mary's voice, Elizabeth recognized that this movement in her womb was different—not a wriggling or squirming, but a jump, a *jump for joy*.

The second question is why did John jump for joy?

I propose that John jumped for joy because the voice he heard gave him a reason to hope: the promise of redemption for all.

Like John then, we are in a womb now. In our life on this earth we await our birth into eternal life. If we listen, listen intently, we too can hear a voice that causes us to jump for joy here and now. We can jump for joy for the same reason that John jumped for joy.

I have tried in this small book to help us listen so that you and I, and all and each one of us, everybody, can jump for joy here and now as we await our birth.

---

[32] Luke: 1, 39-45

Our Destiny

It is not hopeless. We are not alone. We have a lover--

Benedict XVI has said[33] that Christians (and Muslims and Jews and Buddhists and Hindus and all the rest of us) have the "duty and privilege to proclaim that the true nature of man is a seeker of God."

Many activities are natural; but only one is really natural:

- It is natural to eat, to itch, to wonder, to seek pleasure, to err, to cry,
- to sleep, to be awake, but above all else it is necessary, it is essential,
- **it is natural** to seek God.

Without God, human development is either denied or is entrusted exclusively to humankind. Either way, our understanding of human development consequently falls into the trap of thinking that humans can bring about their own fulfillment.

And that is simply not so.

If there is no prospect of eternal life, human progress risks being reduced to the accumulation of wealth, honors, gratification, sensual delights, political influence, and other ultimately useless endeavors.

But we are God's creation. We are not lost atoms in a random universe.

He has always loved us. He loved us before we existed. He loves us now. He will always love us, no matter what we do, no matter what happens to us. Because of his love he has endowed each of us with an immortal soul. That is why it will become better than this—every

---

[33] Upon his arrival in Israel in May, 2009.

person possesses a nature that is destined to transcend itself in a supernatural life.

I have attempted to show that for any significant topic we might wish to discuss, there is more to that topic than we might at first realize. It is also true that whatever we may consider our life to be, there also is more than we might at first realize. Whatever our condition may be, it could be better than what we are now experiencing.

Like this:

Isaiah in Chapter 54, and all the other prophets, over and over again and again keep saying:

> God's love for us makes Him *appear* to be foolish, foolish because He knows we will blow it, and we have proven Him right: We do fall into sin again and again and again, and He forgives us over and over; until finally, you might say in His exasperation, He redeems us and takes us into His bosom. He takes us like a loving mother would take us, into Heaven, because there in Heaven we can no longer refuse to love Him.
>
> We will instead love Him fully and completely.

He might seem to be distant, vengeful, and generally terrifying. He is all that—and more. We need to understand that this terrifying God is our lover. When we understand this a little bit, we will also better understand His love, and why He redeemed us.

Before we existed he knew in advance that we would need help in our weakness. So, because of His great love for us, God the Father decided that he would send His Son to us so that we could be redeemed. So, he created the universe and put us in it and sent his son who redeemed us.

So here we are, all redeemed and everything, and I hope I understand all this and act on it, and you too do the same, because we are being continually immersed in His love for us and that is what is really terrifying about our loving, foolish Creator.

> Now, having been loved before there was anything, then created, and now redeemed by His Son, Jesus Christ, who

has made us aware of His indescribably great love through His life and especially by His sacrifice on the cross and His resurrection, we can with the help of the Holy Spirit and in community with others here and now do our best to freely love God without condition and everybody else the same way also. (It ain't easy to do all that fellow-man loving.) Meanwhile we do the best we can looking forward with rejoicing and hope to our eternal life with the Triune Trinity.

Be well, and live righteously!

Appendix

<u>Beyond the Rainbow—</u>

In my opinion, when introducing a complex topic it is more important to get the essence across to the listener than it is to discuss the details, especially when it appears that the details could impede communication of the essence. Accordingly, I have omitted any discussion of Fraunhofer absorption lines in the spectra of the stars.

<u>Water—</u>

Regarding those bricks:

Laid flat, a typical brick is 4.50 inches wide and 8.62 inches long. The area of that flat surface is 0.269 square feet:

(4.50 in. × 8.62 in.)/144 sq. in./sq. ft. = 0.269 sq. ft.

The surface area of a sphere $= \pi \times (\text{diameter})^2$. For simplicity, the earth is taken to be a sphere with a diameter of 8000 miles and a corresponding surface area of 2.01×10^8 sq. mi. or 5.60×10^{15} sq. ft. That is, for the earth, the surface area is

$$\pi \times (8.00 \times 10^3)^2 \text{ sq. mi.} = 3.14 \times 6.40 \times 10^7 \text{ sq. mi.} = 2.01 \times 10^8 \text{ sq. mi.}$$

There are $(5.28 \times 10^3)^2$ square feet in one square mile. So for the earth, the surface area in square feet is 5.60×10^{15}.

That is, in 2.01×10^8 sq. mi. there are 5.60×10^{15} square feet.

2.01×10^8 *sq. mi.* $\times (5.28 \times 10^3)^2$ *sq. ft./sq. mi.* $= 5.60 \times 10^{15}$ *sq. ft.*

At 0.27 sq. ft per brick, 2.1×10^{16} bricks are necessary to cover the 5.60×10^{15} square feet of the earth with one layer of bricks.

5.60 X10^{15} sq. ft./0.27 sq. ft./brick = 2.1 X 10^{16} bricks

Now for the thousand planets we will need the calculation goes like this:

21,000,000,000,000,000 bricks × 1000 is approximately equal to 20,000,000,000,000,000,000 bricks:

Or, using tens with exponents:

2.10 × 10^{16} bricks × 1.00 × 10^3 ~ 2 X 10^{19} bricks

In other words, when we have 2 X 10^{19} bricks, we will need one thousand earth-sized planets if each planet is to be completely covered with one layer of bricks.

For the number of clusters in a glass of water:

Assume a 6 ounce glass of water containing liquid water that is composed of clusters, each cluster containing six water molecules.

At 28.3 g/oz., 18.0 g/mole, 6.00 molecules per cluster, and 6.20 X 10^{23} molecules/mole:

For the number of moles of water in six ounces of water.

6.00oz × 28.3 g/oz. = 170 g.

So 170 g/18 g/mole = 9.43 moles

For the number of clusters, each with six molecules of water, in 9.43 moles of water.

6.02 X 10^{23} molecules/mole × 9.43 moles/6.00 molecules/cluster = 9.46 × 10^{23} ≈ 1 × 10^{24} clusters

Snowflake

Snowflakes vary in size and shape. Consider the hexagonally symmetrical crystalline snowflakes that are pictured in books and, from time to time, in newspaper articles. Approximately, one million of such snowflakes weigh one ounce, or, same thing, 28.3 grams[34].

---

[34] Ten pennies weigh approximately 30 grams so 9 pennies plus a skimpy half of a penny would weigh about 28.3 grams.

There are 602,000,000,000,000,000,000,000 molecules[35] of water in eighteen grams of water.

Therefore, in 28.3 grams of water there are

28.3 grams of water $\times$ 6.02 $\times$ 10^{23} molecules of water $\div$ 1 / 18.0 grams of water $\approx$ 10 $\times$ 10^{23} molecules of water.

That is, the group of approximately one million snowflakes that weigh one ounce is composed of 10 $\times$ 10^{23} molecules of water.

Consequently, in one snowflake there are approximately

10 $\times$ 10^{23} molecules of water $\div$ 10^{6} = 10 $\times$ 10^{17} molecules of water in one snowflake.

That is 1,000,000,000,000,000,000 molecules, in an average crystalline snowflake.

---

[35] 602 sextillion molecules.